Margaret Roberts

◆ LITTLE BOOK OF ◆

LAVENDER

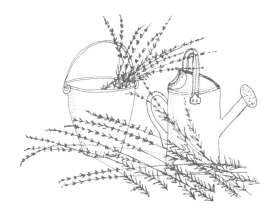

ISBN 1 86812 672 2

First edition, first impression 1997

Published by Southern Book Publishers (Pty) Ltd
PO Box 3103, Halfway House, 1685

Design and DTP by Tracey Mackenzie
Set in 10 on 12 point Palatino
Cover photograph by Cath Simpson
Illustrations by Margaret Roberts
Printed and bound by National Book Printers,
Drukkery Street, Goodwood, Western Cape

Contents

Origins

The name lavender comes originally from the Latin word *lavare*, which means to wash, and it is one of those esteemed ancient herbs that was first used, perhaps due to its refreshing scent, to cleanse clothes, furnishings and for baths.

Centuries ago, strong-smelling herbs known as 'strewing herbs' were scattered over floors to keep the air fresh smelling and to mask the pungent smells of open sewers and drains. Lavender would have been much esteemed as a strewing herb, owing to its marvellous antiseptic, deodorant and insect-repelling properties.

One of the earliest recordings of lavender was made by the Greek writer, Dioscorides. His authoritative list of the earliest medicinal plants compiled in the first century AD recorded *Lavandula stoechas*, commonly known today as Spanish lavender. His recommendations were to boil the flower heads in water as this brew was believed to be 'good for ye griefs in ye thorax'.

There is a great deal of folklore surrounding it in many countries, where it is still used in the same way as it was many hundreds of years ago.

Lavender in its many forms grows wild in many warm countries of the world, and is perhaps the world's favourite herb. Its habitats are fascinating. It is mainly indigenous to the Mediterranean region, where it thrives in semi-desert conditions with light, sandy soils and hot sun.

Varieties that have high oil yields have been introduced into Russia, Australia, America, Canada, Britain, Japan, Holland, Germany, Belgium and Bulgaria, where the lavenders have become commercial crops.

Growing lavender

L avender propagation can become an all-absorbing hobby and with the exquisite fragrance and marvellously decorative and therapeutic qualities of lavender, it is not difficult to become as obsessed as I have over the years with growing this wonderful herb in its many beautiful varieties.

All lavenders need full sun in order to produce their gloriously rich oils. They thrive in hot weather in the baking sun and do best in light, sandy, well-drained soil. Most species can take the cold, a fair amount of frost, and have a fairly long life. I find the need to replace them every 4 to 5 years, as they tend to become woody and overgrown, but if they are kept clipped they look beautiful for 6 or 7 years.

Lavender grows beautifully in tubs and large pots, and clipping and pruning back after flowering will ensure uniform growth. Clip back roughly ¼ of the bush, more or less level with the base of the flower stem, and remove any dead parts. Remember that although it usually needs sandy, well-drained soil, in a tub or big pot it will need extra watering and feeding. Dig in compost to your potting soil mixture and check that the drainage holes are open and clear of debris. Remember to stand the tub in full sun and turn it every month to ensure even growth. Add a natural fertiliser three times a year in spring, midsummer and autumn to ensure continuous flowering.

Lavender does well with a deep weekly watering, making it a superb plant for waterwise gardening in our hot country.

> **HANDY HINT**
> Fresh lavender flowers and sprinklings of lavender oil keep rats and mice away.

Soil preparation

Dig a hole 40 x 40 cm. Mix 1 bucket river sand to 2 buckets garden soil and ½ bucket compost. (If the soil is generally well drained and light, omit the sand — just dig in the compost.) Place the lavender in the hole resting on the mixed soil. Fill with water and then press down more soil and make a basin or 'dam' around it.

To retain the moisture in the soil, add a light mulch of leaves and grass around the plant. Use only organic gardening methods — no chemical fertilisers or sprays — so you can use your plant for medicinal and cosmetic purposes.

Seed sowing

Lavender propagates easily by sowing the tiny black seeds in wet, sandy trays. Sprinkle carefully and cover lightly with sieved sand. Cover the tray with a sheet of glass and keep it in a shady place. Check daily to see if the sand is still damp — it must never dry out at this critical stage. Water gently with the finest spray and keep under the glass covering until the little seedlings become sturdy.

Gradually, as they reach 4 to 5 cm in height, prick out the seedlings and plant them in bags with compost mixed into the sandy soil. Keep the soil moist but not wet, and gradually move them out into the sun for short periods, until they are sturdy enough to stand out all day. Let them establish well in the bags before planting them out in the garden.

When planting out, remember that lavenders need space — no less than 1 metre between each one — and the big lavenders, *Lavandula angustifolia* and *L. latifolia*, need 2 metres.

PROPAGATION BY CUTTINGS

My most successful propagations have been cuttings from the mother plant, with careful tags recording the date and mother stock. Three seasons later the results have been wonderful.

Certainly the easiest way to increase your stock of lavender is by cuttings. Pull off a 4–6 cm sprig from the main stem, leaving the little heel attached, and strip off the lower leaves. Make a hole with a stick a little bigger than the stem in a deep tray of wet sand. Press in the cutting and firm well. Do this row by row, leaving 3 cm between each one. Place the full tray in a shady, protected spot and keep moist.

The best time to take cuttings is in spring and autumn. In autumn place the trays under cover (make mini greenhouses under thick, clear plastic or place the trays in a warm, light greenhouse or sunfilled room during winter).

Once they have rooted, gently prick them out, being extra careful not to disturb the tender little roots. Plant them into bags filled with compost and moist sand and keep them watered until they are strong enough to go out gradually into the sun to harden off. Plant the cuttings out once they have bushed out to 3 or 4 times their original size. They need to be sturdy, tough and acclimatised to the outdoors before they find their permanent home in the garden in full sun.

To harden off a cutting place the bag in morning sun for 1 hour the first day, 2 hours the second, 3 hours the third and 4 hours the fourth day. For the next week place the bag in morning sun for 5-6 hours and thereafter you'll find the little plant quite tough. On hot afternoons give it a sprinkling of water and place the plant in dappled shade if it looks wilted. Plant out in the garden on a cool, rainy day or in late afternoon

Varieties

L avender belongs to the great family or
genus Labiatae. Amongst other family
members are the sages, origanums, thymes,
mints, basils and savories, easily identified by
their rich — often pungent — fragrance and the
small, two-lipped mauve, white and sometimes
pink flowers that appear between bracts, and
the rather angular or square stems.

As with all the Labiates, hybridisation
amongst the lavenders is common, which
means there is a large degree of confusion with
naming and cataloguing. Lavender's hybrids
arise mainly by insect pollination — notice how
bees and butterflies dance around those bushes.
A hybrid is a cross between two different
species, or two different varieties that belong
to the same genus. Wild forms are called
'varieties' and cultivated forms are 'cultivars',
and all can be propagated by cuttings. Seed
may revert to one or other parent, or come up
with something new!

SPANISH LAVENDER *Lavandula stoechas*

Usually called Spanish lavender, sometimes Italian and occasionally French lavender, *L. stoechas* is distinctive for its handsome dark purply-pink flowers and brilliant dark purple or magenta bracts that decorate the top of the tight 4-sided cone-like flowers. It is infinitely desirable as a garden subject. I have grown the taller variety, which only has a spring flowering period, and it is a show stopper! It should be clipped back neatly as it can reach 1 metre in height and tends to straggle rather untidily.

A smaller, more compact version has become increasingly available through the nurseries lately, commonly called miniature Spanish lavender. This has a smaller, more purple flower and a longer flowering period, with a smaller flush of flowers again in autumn. It forms a neat round bush about ½ a metre in height and can be clipped into excellent shapes as it does not topple or sprawl at all, but forms a mass of delicate foliage.

The leaves of both varieties are small and slender with straight edges and although, when fresh, they have a typical camphorish lavender scent and they make excellent pot pourri additions, the plant is no longer medicinally used.

Spanish lavender

FRENCH LAVENDER
Lavandula dentata

Commonly known as French lavender, fringed lavender or toothed lavender, this is a favourite garden subject, and can be easily identified by the tiny indentations on the leaves — hence the species name *dentata*.

There are two commonly found varieties: one is a smaller-leaved, smaller-flowered variety with green leaves, and the other is *L. dentata* var. *candicans*, which has grey leaves and larger flowers. Both flower continuously and the lovely light mauve, cone-like flowers with the typically large 'petals' or coma on the tip make excellent cut flowers, tied in tight bundles, or dried for pot pourris. Once dried they do not really retain much scent, but they do retain much of their colour and look pretty in pot pourris.

Kept carefully trimmed, these lavenders with their long flowering period look attractive as a border for paths and make neat low hedges.

French lavender

ENGLISH LAVENDER *Lavandula angustifolia*

The richly aromatic English lavenders encompass many cultivars and varieties owing to many prolific years of natural hybridisation, not only in their native habitat.

Within this range are all the smooth, narrow, grey-green leaved lavenders with long flowering heads with whorls of tiny flowers along the stem. These include such names as *L.a. vera, L.a. munstead, L.a. hidcote* and *L.a. nana,* which is a dwarf lavender, sometimes with white flowers (*L.a. nana alba*).

The *angustifolias* have the strongest scents of all the lavenders. They were grown worldwide from the sixteenth century for their high oil yields and were introduced into the perfume industry. Mitchum's lavender was one of the first in England and my grandmother was familiar with what she called 'Mitchum's old English spike lavender', an old-fashioned cushion of long velvety grey leaves and a typical candelabra-type flowering spray indicating its *L. angustifolia* and *L. latifolia* ancestry. The scent is distinctly camphor-like — very strong — and although it is one of the hybrids between *L. angustifolia, L. latifolia* and possibly *L. lanata,* which has woolly stems and leaves, it stands alone as the true old English lavender, much loved in English cottage gardens. My grandmother brought it from her home in Scotland, as the seeds are very easily germinated.

On these bushes she dried her linen on wash days, especially underwear, pillow cases and handkerchiefs, and used boiled lavender water as the final rinse to impart its nostalgic fragrance. I have named this **Grandmother's old English lavender** in the nursery trade, and think of her every time I see it or smell that deep, nose-clearing scent. It always reminds me of the little posies and sachets she taught us to make in our childhood.

Many flowering stalks are borne all summer long and these, and the leaves, can be dried for sachets. They will retain their scent for years and years.

Giant English lavender, also commonly called **true English lavender,** is a wonderful huge tough bush that grows to 1½ metres in height and width and is covered all year round with long spikes of flowers on single, unbranched stems. The flowers are densely packed on the stem tips and then in whorls lower down the stem with spaces between them.

Bunches of the richly fragrant leaves and flowers are wonderful in the vase — a florist's delight — and I constantly wonder why it is not grown more widely in South Africa for cut flowers. Its scent is so astonishing in a room and dried it is best of all for pot pourris, colognes and sachets.

Kept clipped and trimmed it does not have to reach such giant proportions and although most lavenders have a tendency for a branch or two to die off, this giant English lavender hardly ever gives a problem. I replace the bushes every 5 years as they become unmanageable.

Small English lavender (*L.a. vera, L.a. munstead* or *L.a. hidcote*) is a compact bush with small grey leaves arranged in fours around the square stem. It is very decorative, richly scented and has bright purple or light mauve and sometimes white flowers.

Clipped and curbed it can retain uniformity and is exquisite in spring and autumn when the bright flowers perkily draw the butterflies. These are the best flowers for retaining their colour, yet do not have as strong a scent as the other *angustifolias*. Plant these smaller varieties ½ a metre apart as they make a neat border and can take clipping in midsummer to keep them compact. Watch for waterlogged soil as they cannot stand 'wet feet'.

BLIND LAVENDER (SPICA LAVENDER) *Lavandula* x *allardii*

This is a giant, sprawling bush with smooth grey leaves, occasionally dentate, and very few flowering spikes. It reaches 2 metres in height and width and is pure fragrant pleasure to make into lavender baths, rinses, lotions and sprays. Give it space, full sun and a deep weekly watering and you'll be amply rewarded! It is the best lavender for making a hedge as it responds to training and clipping (clip back to the base of the flower stems) and has no tendency to die off unless it is neglected.

Blind lavender

The name *spica* is now obsolete. Linnaeus, the Swedish botanist, identified *L. angustifolia* and *L. latifolia* as varieties of the same species and named them *L. spica*, a name which over the years came to be regarded as too ambiguous and so was deleted. But 'spica lavender' has stuck as a common name and this great beauty is still referred to by this name, which confuses the nurserymen! It is probably safest to call it blind lavender.

The scent is strongly camphor-like and has lingering effects. Simmering it in boiling water will clear cooking or pet smells in the room, and laying sprigs under carpets will get rid of fishmoths and ants as it releases antiviral oils into the atmosphere. A bowl of lightly bruised sprigs will clear the air in a sickroom.

DUTCH LAVENDER *L. angustifolia* x *dentata* or *L. latifolia* x *L. dentata*

This is a compact, tough, 70 cm to 1 metre high bush with leaves that are dense, grey, soft and dentate and the largest of all lavender leaves. It has a few flowers occasionally, but its real beauty is in the shape and the denseness of the bush.

I have grown a row of Dutch lavender 2 metres apart, from which I have clipped, picked and dried the fragrant leaves as the base for all my pot pourris and cosmetics. Owing to the frequent clippings, cuttings and prunings the bushes have never got out of hand and with their prolific growth I have had an endless supply. They remain a superb garden subject and have grown vigorously for 6 years now without dying back at all.

Recently, a visitor from Holland told me that this lavender grew quite extensively near his home town in the early part of the century and as it had such a high oil yield, it was used commercially to scent furniture polish.

Dutch lavender

FERN-LEAF LAVENDER *Lavandula canariensis*

Originally from the Canary Islands, this lavender has only in recent years been introduced to South Africa, where it flourishes. The delicate, tender, rare and exquisite leaves are strangely unlike those of the other lavenders. They are light green, glossy and bipinnate, with a fern-like appearance. The bush grows to about 1 metre in height, and the flowering spike is tall, with long, narrow, small deep purple flowers in tiny bracts, often branching. In mid July they are already dazzling in their colour and attraction to bees.

Virtually scentless, it is nevertheless a fascinating garden subject and often has flowers throughout the year. These last well in vases and quickly set seed that germinates easily. In fact, once you have one bush of fern-leaf lavender, tiny seedlings will pop up everywhere. Cuttings are equally easy to strike.

I have found this to be a most charming pot plant subject in a large, well-drained pot on a patio, in full sun. All that is needed is a tidying up of the dry leaves that tend to hang under the new growth and a good clipping back twice yearly to keep it looking good. I trim mine into perfect ball shapes and with the mass of purple flowers above the foliage, it is very pretty indeed. I replace the old bushes every 3 to 5 years as they tend to become woody and sparsely flowered as they age.

WOOLLY LAVENDER *Lavandula multifida*

This variety is similar to the fern-leaf lavender but is smaller in growth and has soft, hairy fern-like leaves and smaller more compact flowers, usually in two shades of purple. The flowering spike is branched into three, candelabra style, and the flowers are scentless. The bush tends to sprawl and is rather untidy. This is one of the more tender lavenders and is fairly difficult to grow.

Cooking
with
lavender

The fact that lavender can be used in cooking always comes as a surprise to anyone who thought lavender was purely for fragrance or cosmetics. Lavender is so versatile and imparts a wonderfully fresh, clean taste to food. The flowers and young leaves are the parts used in cooking and I find the giant English lavender and Grandmother's old English lavender the most delicious in recipes, as neither taste of camphor, despite their strong camphor-like scent.

EQUIVALENT MEASUREMENTS

1 teaspoon = 5 ml
1 tablespoon = 15 ml
1 cup = 250 ml

Starters

These can be served with drinks before a meal. Their fresh taste makes them the ideal start to a rich meal.

LAVENDER CROUTONS
Serves 6

about 4 slices of bread
sunflower oil
2 tablespoons lavender leaves and flowers, finely chopped

Slice the bread in small, neat fingers. Heat a little sunflower oil in a pan and add the lavender leaves and flowers and the bread fingers. Stir gently with a spatula until lightly browned, drain on crumpled kitchen paper towel and serve hot with dips.

AVOCADO AND LAVENDER DIP
Serves 6–8

1 large or 2 small ripe avocados
lemon juice
salt and coarsely ground black pepper
1 tablespoon lavender leaves, finely chopped
parsley, finely chopped

Mash the avocado with the lemon juice, salt and pepper. Add the lavender leaves and mix well. Sprinkle with parsley and serve with croutons or crisps.

LAVENDER CHEESE SQUARES
Serves 6

6 slices brown bread
butter
½ – ¾ cup mayonnaise
2 teaspoons lavender leaves and flowers, finely chopped
about 1½ cups mozzarella cheese
cayenne pepper

Toast slices of brown bread and butter while still hot. Mix the chopped lavender into the mayonnaise and spread onto the toast. Grate mozzarella cheese, sprinkle on top of the lavender mayonnaise and dust with cayenne pepper. Place under the grill and grill lightly for 4 minutes or until the cheese melts and bubbles and starts to brown. Cut into squares. Serve hot with sherry.

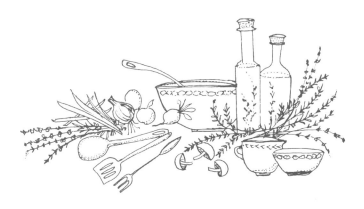

Soups

I find lavender is best with pale soups, and it seems to go especially well with cucumber and celery, onions, potato and turnips.

POTATO, LEEK AND LAVENDER SOUP

Serves 6–8
This is a real winter warmer and filling enough to be a meal on its own served with thick crusty bread.

3 tablespoons butter
about 6 leeks, well washed and thinly sliced
6 large potatoes, peeled and diced
4 cups chicken stock
sea salt
black pepper
1 tablespoon young lavender leaves, finely chopped
4 cups milk

In a large heavy pot melt the butter and add the leeks. Brown lightly. Add the potatoes and coat with the buttery mixture. Stir fry for a minute or two. Add all the other ingredients except the milk and simmer until the leeks and potatoes are tender. Liquidise and then return it all to the pot, add the milk and simmer for 5 minutes. Sprinkle with chopped parsley, a few lavender flowers and a dash of nutmeg and serve hot with croutons.

> **❧ HANDY HINT**
> When your hands smell of the onion you've been chopping, rub them vigorously with lavender sprigs.

JERUSALEM ARTICHOKE AND LAVENDER SOUP

Serves 8

Tasty and nutritious, this soup is much loved in Europe during autumn when artichokes are plentiful.

500 g fresh Jerusalem artichokes
juice of 2–3 lemons
2 large onions, finely chopped
½ cup sunflower cooking oil
2 small turnips, peeled and grated
1½ litres chicken stock or water
1 tablespoon lavender leaves, finely chopped
2 tablespoons mint, finely chopped
1 tablespoon fennel seed or stalk and leaves, finely chopped
salt and cayenne pepper to taste
150 ml cream

Dice the artichokes and toss in lemon juice to prevent discolouration. Meanwhile brown the onion in the oil. Add the turnips and brown lightly. Add the artichokes and turn everything together well. Add the stock. Simmer for 20 minutes or until the artichokes are soft. Liquidise and return to the pot. Add all the other ingredients, stir well and simmer for a further 3–6 minutes. Either cool and refrigerate and serve chilled, or sprinkle with mint and lavender flowers and serve hot.

Fish dishes

The fresh taste of lavender lends itself wonderfully well to fish dishes and I find myself reaching for the lavender whenever I prepare fish.

LAVENDER AND HAKE STIR FRY
Serves 4

6 hake fillets, skinned and sliced
a little oil
1 large onion, thinly sliced
1 green pepper, diced
1 cup cabbage, thinly sliced
juice of 1 lemon
2 potatoes, thinly sliced
sea salt
freshly ground black pepper
1 tablespoon parsley, chopped
2 tablespoons fennel leaves, chopped
½ tablespoon lavender leaves and flowers, chopped

Brown the fish in oil in a frying pan or wok. Add the onion and green pepper and brown lightly. Then add the cabbage, lemon juice and potatoes. Add more oil if necessary. Add sea salt and pepper and the finely chopped herbs. Stir briskly until the potatoes are cooked.

Serve hot on brown rice, with fresh lemon wedges. Decorate with lavender flowers and fennel sprigs.

BAKED FISH WITH LAVENDER SAUCE

Serves 4–6

This is my favourite supper dish when everyone is late and tired. It's quick, easy and appetising.

6 portions of any fish, skinned and deboned
2 onions, thinly sliced
1 cup celery stalks and leaves, chopped
1 cup carrots, thinly diced
salt
black pepper
lemon juice
1 tablespoon lavender leaves and flowers, chopped
chopped parsley
Sauce
2½ cups milk
2 eggs
2 tablespoons cornflour
1 cup grated cheese

Set the oven to 180 °C. Place the fish portions in a baking dish and scatter the onions over the fish. Add the celery stalks and leaves, and carrots, scattering evenly. Sprinkle with salt, pepper and lemon juice. Set aside while you make the sauce.

To make the sauce, whisk the milk with the eggs and cornflour. Add the grated cheese and stir in well. Pour over the fish. Sprinkle over this the lavender leaves and flowers and bake at 180 °C for 20–25 minutes or until it is lightly brown on top and bubbly. Sprinkle with chopped parsley and serve piping hot with mashed potato and a salad.

BRAAIED FISH WITH LAVENDER AND ROSEMARY

Serves 4–6

This is most delicious with a whole fish that has been cleaned and trimmed, or you can use large fillets.

6–8 fish fillets
2 apples, peeled and quartered
2 onions, thinly sliced
1 sprig lavender
1 sprig rosemary
1 tablespoon crushed coriander seeds
sea salt
black pepper
2 tablespoons butter
fresh lemon juice

Place the fish in a large double piece of tin foil. Arrange the apples, onions and herbs around and on top of it. Sprinkle with salt and pepper. Dot with butter and squeeze the lemon juice over everything. Fold up well and place over the coals. Turn the parcel over from time to time to ensure even cooking. Check the fish after 15 minutes, but cooking it a little longer will allow a delicious sauce to develop. Discard the rosemary and lavender sprigs, tuck in fresh sprigs to decorate and serve hot.

Wrap potatoes in foil and tuck them into the coals to bake with the fish. Add a squeeze or two of lemon juice and butter to the baked potatoes when serving.

> **❧ HANDY HINT**
> Offer finger bowls of lavender water with fruit or shellfish. Boil lavender in enough water to cover for 10 minutes, cool and strain.

Main dishes

As lavender is so beneficial for gastric ailments, particularly flatulence, and helps to tenderise tough meat, it seems a natural ingredient in casseroles, stews and braised meat dishes. The antispasmodic properties in lavender help break down and digest fatty meats and assist the liver in its processing. With these remarkable properties, lavender surely deserves more recognition as an important culinary herb.

BEEF AND LAVENDER CASSEROLE

Serves 6
Lavender aids the digestion of this nourishing winter casserole.

little cooking oil
2 large onions, sliced
1 kg rump steak, thinly sliced
2 tablespoons flour
2 celery sticks, sliced
6 carrots, peeled and diced
2 green peppers, sliced
4 large tomatoes, peeled and sliced
4 large potatoes, peeled and diced
sea salt, cayenne pepper to taste
2 tablespoons brown sugar
1 tablespoon fresh thyme
1 tablespoon fresh lavender leaves
2 teaspoons coriander seeds, crushed
juice of 1 lemon

In a large heavy iron pot, brown the onions in the oil. Roll the meat in the flour, then add to the onions and brown. Add all the other ingredients and enough water to cover. Put the lid on and either simmer on top of the stove or bake at 180 °C until tender. Serve with brown rice and green beans.

BRAAIED PORK CHOPS WITH LAVENDER AND HONEY

Serves 4

4 pork chops, trimmed of excess fat
Marinade
salt and cayenne pepper to taste
juice of 2 lemons
1 tablespoon fresh lavender leaves, chopped
3 tablespoons honey
pinch of cloves
sprinkle of fennel seed

Mix all the marinade ingredients together. Pour into a screw-top jar and shake. Pour over the chops and turn them in it. Refrigerate overnight. The next day place everything in a roasting pan and grill either in the oven or on the coals. Baste frequently with the marinade and cook until golden and tender. Serve with grilled tomatoes, mashed potato and green peas.

LAVENDER CHICKEN BREASTS

Serves 4–6

Lavender seems to make poultry extra rich and succulent and this easily made dish is sure to become a firm favourite.

4 large chicken breasts, cut in half lengthways
2 onions, peeled and sliced
2 cups coarse brown breadcrumbs mixed with
  1 cup chopped celery
  juice of 1 lemon
  1 tablespoon Vital brewer's yeast or Mega yeast
  1 tablespoon fresh thyme leaves
  sea salt and cayenne pepper
  ½ tablespoon fresh lavender leaves, chopped
  1 cup plain yoghurt

Lay the chicken breasts in a baking dish. Cover with onion rings and then spoon over the breadcrumb and yoghurt mixture. Dot with butter and bake covered until tender, for about 25 minutes. Remove the cover and brown lightly under the grill. Serve hot with baked potatoes and peas.

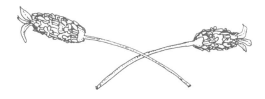

Vegetarian main dishes

L avender is a wonderful complement to pulses and pasta as it
is so refreshing and an excellent digestive.

STUFFED MARROW WITH LAVENDER
Serves 6

little oil
2 cups sliced mushrooms
salt and pepper
1 tablespoon fresh lavender leaves, chopped
2 cups brown breadcrumbs
2 onions, finely chopped
salt and cayenne pepper to taste
1 medium-sized marrow
2 tablespoons skim milk powder
lemon juice

Sauté the mushrooms in a little oil with the salt and pepper and
the lavender leaves. Add the breadcrumbs and sauté. Finally add
the onions and sauté further. Season with salt and cayenne
pepper. Cut off one end of the squash and remove the pips. Stuff
the hollow inside with the mushroom mixture, the skim milk
powder and a good squeeze of lemon juice. Prop the end in place
with toothpicks. Place on a baking tray, surround with peeled
potatoes and carrots, dot with a little butter and tuck a lavender
sprig under the squash. Cover and roast until tender. Slice and
serve hot, on a bed of brown rice and peas.

LAVENDER AND BUTTER BEAN PIE

Serves 6–8

The lavender and mint in this filling dish help with flatulence and the gassiness of the beans is removed by discarding the first water and boiling them up again in fresh water.

1 kg butter beans soaked overnight and washed
2 onions, sliced into rings
little oil
1 teaspoon Marmite dissolved in about 150 ml hot water
2 cups grated cheese
½ kg potatoes, boiled and mashed with butter, salt and pepper,
  a little milk and 1 beaten egg
1 tablespoon chopped lavender leaves

Boil the beans in water for 5 minutes, discard the water and boil up again in fresh water until tender (about 1 hour). Sauté the onions in the oil until lightly browned. Spoon a layer of beans and onions into an ovenproof dish, pour over the Marmite mixture, and top with half of the cheese. Spread with mashed potatoes, sprinkle with the chopped lavender and finally sprinkle with the rest of the cheese. Dot with butter and bake at 180 °C for 20 minutes or until golden.

LAVENDER RISOTTO
Serves 6

1 kg broccoli or green vegetable in season
1 large onion, diced
1 clove garlic, crushed
salt and pepper
2 teaspoons fresh lavender leaves, chopped
2 cups cooked brown rice
Sauce
2 tablespoons butter
2 tablespoons flour
1¾ cups (400 ml) vegetable stock or milk
2 beaten eggs
sea salt and freshly ground black pepper
2–3 tablespoons tomato paste
breadcrumbs
mozzarella cheese

Wash and shred the vegetables. Cook in a little water with the garlic and a knob of butter and the salt, pepper and the lavender. Cover and cook until tender — about 6–7 minutes. Pour the vegetables into an ovenproof dish, mixed with the cooked rice.

To make the sauce, melt the butter, add the flour, stir well and then add the stock or milk mixed with the beaten eggs, salt, pepper and tomato paste. Stir as it begins to thicken. Pour the sauce over the vegetables, sprinkle with breadcrumbs and a little grated mozzarella cheese. Dot with butter, bake at 180 °C for 15–20 minutes. Serve with a salad and crusty bread, or lavender cheese squares (see p. 15).

Desserts

The fragrantly fresh, palate-cleansing flavour of lavender lends itself beautifully to desserts.

LAVENDER FRUIT SALAD

Serves 6
Use any mixed fresh fruit, to make about 6 cups. My favourite is green honeydew melon made into balls.

1 cup mango or litchi juice
2 sprigs lavender
sliced fresh peaches or mangoes
green honeydew melon, made into balls
granadilla pulp
strawberries cut in halves

Warm the mango or litchi juice with the sprigs of lavender for 5 minutes, then discard the lavender sprigs. Pour this over the fruit (sprinkle very tart fruit with lavender sugar or lavender honey first). Strip a lavender stalk of its tender young flowers and sprinkle over the whole fruit salad.

Serve with lavender sprigs tucked under the bowl or on the saucer of each individual dessert dish or fill the scooped out melon halves and place on a bed of lavender. On a hot summer evening, tuck crushed ice around the melon halves.

> ❧ HANDY HINT
> Twist a spray of lavender flowers together and tuck them into your sugar bowl to scent the sugar.

Lavender meringues

Serves 12

6 egg whites
3 tablespoons fresh lavender flowers
3 tablespoons castor sugar
2½ cups white sugar
4 teaspoons baking powder
Lavender cream
1 carton cream
1 tablespoon lavender flowers
3 tablespoons castor sugar

Whisk the egg whites in a clean bowl until stiff. In another bowl, crush the lavender flowers with the castor sugar and add the white sugar. Add the baking powder and stir until well mixed. Gradually add to the whisked egg whites, a little at a time. Fold in gently and lightly with a metal spoon.

Cover a baking tray with baking paper or double folded brown paper and place a tablespoon of meringue mixture at a time neatly in rows on the paper at least 3 cm apart. Bake in a cool oven (100 °C) for 10–12 hours or overnight. I usually switch off the oven for the last 3–4 hours.

To make the lavender cream, whisk the cream until thick, then add the lavender flowers and castor sugar. Sandwich the meringues together with the cream, decorate with sprigs of lavender and serve with lavender tea.

> ❧ HANDY HINT
> Lavender tea made with
> ¼ cup fresh leaves and
> flowers and left to infuse in
> boiling water for 5 minutes
> will soothe you to sleep.

LEMON AND LAVENDER TART

Not only is this delicious tart refreshing and light, but it is fool-proof, quick and easy.

Pastry
125 g wholewheat flour
pinch of salt
85 g butter
Filling
juice of 3 large lemons
about 3 teaspoons grated lemon rind
3 eggs
150 g castor sugar
150 ml cream
1 tablespoon lavender flowers

Sift the flour and salt into a large bowl and grate in the butter on a coarse grater. Rub briefly together until a soft dough is formed. Pat out into a 20 cm baking dish, pressing up the sides a little. Bake at 180 °C for about 10 minutes or until the pastry is lightly golden and crisp.

To make the filling, grate the rind into a bowl and mix with the juice. In a separate bowl beat the eggs and sugar and add the cream. Whisk until smooth. Add to the lemon juice and rind. Whisk until smooth. Add the lavender flowers last, pour into the pastry case and bake at 140 °C for about 40 minutes or until it is firm. Serve chilled with whipped cream decorated with lavender flowers.

STRAWBERRY AND LAVENDER CHEESE CAKE

Crust
1 packet plain digestive biscuits
175 g melted butter
Filling
175 g castor sugar
2 teaspoons vanilla
3 eggs, separated
juice and rind of 1 lemon
1 tablespoon fresh lavender flowers
500 g chunky plain cream cheese
150 ml thick cream

about 3 cups strawberries, sliced
1 cup redcurrant jelly

To make the crust, crush the biscuits with a rolling pin. Mix well with the melted butter and press into a 20 cm cake tin with a loose, well-oiled base lined with greaseproof paper. Chill.

For the filling, whisk the sugar, vanilla and egg yolks. Mix in the lemon juice, rind, lavender flowers and cream cheese. Whisk the cream and in another bowl whisk the egg whites. Fold both into the cream cheese mixture gently with a metal spoon. Pour into the chilled biscuit base. Bake at 140 °C for 40–60 minutes or until set. Set aside to cool.

Once the cake is cool, pack the strawberries in circles on top and sprinkle with a little brown sugar. Melt the redcurrant jelly in a small saucepan and gently pour this glaze over the fruit. Allow to cool and decorate with a sprig of lavender.

LAVENDER ICE-CREAM

Serves 6–8

I have served this exquisite ice-cream at a dinner party with lavender shortbread and it has never been forgotten!

2 cups milk
2 tablespoons fresh lavender flowers
2 eggs
250 g castor sugar
2 tablespoons cornflour mixed with a little milk
2 full cups thick cream, well beaten
touch of mauve food colouring (optional)

Warm the milk and the lavender flowers in a saucepan. Beat the eggs with the sugar until creamy, and add to the milk with the cornflour mixture slowly and carefully, beating constantly with a wooden spoon. Once it has thickened, stand covered and cool. Fold in the cream and food colouring if desired and pour into freezer trays. Place in the freezer for 1 hour, remove and spoon into a large bowl, beat well and return to the freezer. Do this once or twice more, then freeze until firm. Beating it up well will break down ice crystals and make it light and spongy.

Serve in glass bowls decorated with lavender sprigs with lavender shortbread.

Baking with lavender

Lavender is a wonderful addition to bread, scones and biscuits. Merely add a tablespoon of lavender flowers to a favourite teatime recipe!

LAVENDER OIL SCONES

Makes 12

This recipe was given to me by a beloved French teacher who lived in Montpelier, France. She gathered the lavender from the hillsides and used it fresh.

2 cups cake and wholewheat flour, mixed
4 teaspoons baking powder
½ teaspoon salt
1 tablespoon lavender flowers
100 ml sunflower cooking oil
2 eggs beaten with 100 ml milk

Mix the cake and wholewheat flour, baking powder and salt and add the lavender flowers. Beat the oil into the milk and egg mixture. Then, with a knife, cut the egg mixture into the flour mixture until it all combines, but do not knead it. Drop spoonfuls of the mixture onto a greased baking tray about 3 cm apart. Bake at 220 °C for 10 minutes or just until they start to turn golden. Serve hot with butter and lavender honey.

> ❧ HANDY HINT
> Sprinkle a little lavender oil and tuck sprigs of lavender behind your books to keep fishmoths away.

LAVENDER CRUMPETS

Makes about 24

These crumpets are so easy to make and are delicious served hot for Sunday tea.

2 cups cake flour
4 teaspoons baking powder
pinch salt
3 eggs, beaten
4 tablespoons sugar
1 cup milk
½ tablespoon fresh lavender flowers
2 tablespoons soft butter

Sift the flour, baking powder and salt twice into a bowl. Whisk the eggs and sugar until light and foamy, then add the milk, lavender flowers and butter. Whisk well, add to the flour mixture and beat until there are no lumps and it forms a smooth batter.

Have a hot, well-oiled griddle or pan ready. Drop a tablespoonful at a time onto it, wait for it to bubble, then flip it over using a spatula. Serve hot with butter and jam or lavender honey, or for a real treat with whipped cream and fresh strawberries.

LAVENDER LOAF

I often bake this quick and delicious loaf, using either a new clay flower pot (approximately 12–15 cm across) or little individual 6 x 10 cm loaf pans.

500 g wholewheat flour
3 teaspoons baking powder
1 teaspoon salt
½ cup sunflower seeds
1 tablespoon fresh lavender flowers
½ cup fresh milk
2 tablespoons honey
2 cups plain yoghurt

Mix all the dry ingredients. Warm the milk, honey and lastly the yoghurt. Add to the flour mixture, stir thoroughly, pour into a well-greased loaf pan, or flower pot, lined with greaseproof paper that is well oiled on both sides. Bake at 180 °C for about 30–40 minutes or until the loaf sounds hollow when tapped. (The little loaf pans take about half the time.) Serve wrapped in a warm kitchen towel with a little bunch of lavender tucked in and lavender butter.

To make lavender butter, mash 1 tablespoon each of chopped parsley and lavender flowers to every cup of butter, and add a pinch of salt.

LAVENDER SHORTBREAD

250 g soft butter
2 cups castor sugar
2 tablespoons lavender flowers
2 tablespoons cornflour
3 cups cake flour

Cream the butter and sugar briskly until light and fluffy. Mix the lavender flowers, cornflour and flour and stir in gradually to the buttery mixture. Mix well with the fingertips to form a smooth, stiff dough. Press into a baking tray, about 2 cm thick. Prick all over with a fork. Bake at 150 °C until firm and lightly golden in colour. Dredge with castor sugar, and cut into squares while still hot. Serve on a plate decorated with lavender flowers with afternoon tea and think of your grandmother!

This shortbread keeps well in an airtight tin.

For the gourmet

LAVENDER VINEGAR

This easy to make, refreshing vinegar is delicious in salads or stir fries, or with fish, pasta and potato chips. Because of the fragrant oils in the lavender you need only make one extraction.

1 bottle white grape or apple cider vinegar
6–8 sprigs lavender flowers

Push the lavender sprigs into the bottle of vinegar and stand the bottle in the sun for 1 week. Give it a daily turn and shake. After the week, strain out the lavender, decant the now fragrant vinegar into a new decorative bottle and add one or two lavender flowers. Date and label.

HERBES DE PROVENCE

2 tablespoons dried origanum
3 tablespoons dried thyme
1 tablespoon dried winter savory
1 tablespoon dried lavender flowers
1 tablespoon dried rosemary
2 tablespoons dried chopped celery

Mix well and keep in a screw-top jar near the stove. Use in casseroles, soups, stews and stir fries. It is particularly delicious with grilled fish, chicken and big black mushrooms. In winter I add 2 tablespoons celery seed as well to give it a different taste in soups. Add 1 tablespoon crushed coriander seeds for a delicious change!

LAVENDER LIQUEUR

This is excellent as an after dinner liqueur, especially during winter, or served over steamed puddings or baked custard.

juice and rind of 6 large sweet oranges
1 litre brandy
2 cups sugar
1 tablespoon lavender flowers

Grate the orange rind on a fine grater. Squeeze out the juice and pour it into a large jar with a screw top. Mix the brandy and sugar together, and add the grated zest and the lavender flowers. Seal well. Give it a good shake and leave it to infuse for no less than 6 weeks. Give it the odd shake during that time. Strain through cheesecloth and pour into a pretty decanter.

LAVENDER SYRUP

This is an excellent cold remedy served warm in winter but also a charming warm weather drink served cold with ice.

4 cups water
2 cups lemon juice, freshly squeezed
2 tablespoons fresh lavender flowers and leaves
3 cups sugar
6 cloves
4 or 5 strips lemon zest

Simmer everything together in a covered saucepan for 10 minutes. Stand aside and leave to cool overnight. Next morning, strain. Serve with iced water for a cooling drink or add a dash of brandy to ½ cup syrup topped up with boiling water as a winter warmer.

LAVENDER HONEY

This is excellent for herb teas, colddrinks and fruit punches and for coughs and sore throats too. I always have a good quantity on hand as it is a great favourite.

500 g bottle of honey
1 cup lavender flowers and leafy sprigs

Push 4 or 5 lavender flowers and sprigs into a bottle of unsolidified fresh honey. Stand the whole jar in a pot of hot water (not boiling) to infuse the oils of the lavender into the honey. Store for a month before using, then strain the honey and discard the flowers and leaves. Leave a flower stem in the honey for quick identification on the kitchen shelf.

Lavender in cosmetics

Because of the healing qualities in lavender the fragrant leaves and flowers make an excellent base for skin and hair care preparations. Lavender has been used for hundreds of years in cosmetics and the modern cosmetic industry today still makes extensive use of lavender extracts.

The strong English lavenders (*Lavandula angustifolia*) are generally the best ones to use for home purposes.

NOTE: For sensitive skins, always test a little of any recipe on the inside of your wrist first. Leave on for 10 minutes to see if there is any allergic reaction.

LAVENDER WATER

Many of our grandmothers used lavender water as a wash for coarse, oily skin. Through the years I have found this simple treatment to be excellent, not only for oily problem skin, but as an astringent (lavender contains tannius), a freshener, toner and — in a spritz bottle — a wonderful summer cooler, sprayed over the face, neck and arms. Perfect for travelling!

1 cup lavender leaves and flowers
4 cups water

Simply boil the lavender leaves and flowers in the water for 10 minutes and allow it to cool. Strain and keep it in the fridge. Dab the skin with pads of cotton wool soaked in it, or use it as a wash.

LAVENDER BATH BAG

Excellent for soothing away stress, tension, anxiety and fatigue.

2 cups fresh lavender (L. angustifolia) *leaves and flowers*
handkerchief, cotton square or drawstring bag

Pack the lavender into the handkerchief, square of fine fabric or a quickly made drawstring bag (choose a soft pure cotton for this). Soak in a hot bath and use the bag or bundle of tied up lavender as a sponge. I rub soap onto it and use it as a fragrant scrub. Once the bath is over, discard the lavender leaves and flowers, rinse out the bag and dry it. Use fresh lavender for each bath.

> ❧ HANDY HINT
> Add a handful or two of fresh lavender to your bath and its soothing scent will help you unwind.

LAVENDER FOOT BATH

This is deodorising, refreshing and wonderful after a hard day on your feet. It will aid the sleep pattern for the elderly, calm restless children and soothe the aches, pains, anxiety and stress of modern day living.

freshly picked lavender sprigs
boiling water
1 cup Epsom salts

Choose a large, shallow basin. Place it on the floor in front of a comfortable chair. Pack in sprigs of freshly picked lavender leaves (I love the Dutch lavender best here), and pour 2 kettles of boiling water over this. Leave to draw and cool until pleasantly warm. Add 1 cup Epsom salts and sit with the feet immersed, resting on the lavender sprigs. Give yourself 10–15 minutes. Wriggle the toes, rub the feet with the lavender sprigs and relax. Briskly towel dry, massage in some lavender cream and put on cotton socks.

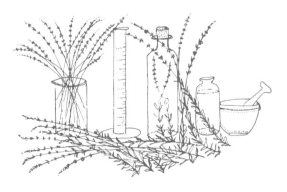

LAVENDER AND OATMEAL SCRUB

2 cups boiling water
2 cups fresh lavender leaves stripped of their stems
  (Grandmother's old English lavender, Dutch lavender
  and blind lavender are superb here)
2 cups coarse oats
1 cup plain yoghurt

In a large saucepan pour the water over the lavender leaves. Leave to draw for 10 minutes. Add oats (I use the big flake non-instant kind), mix in well and press down in the hot lavender water. Heat gently for 5 minutes, then cool to a comfortably warm temperature. Add the yoghurt. Mix well, stand in the bath and taking handfuls at a time, rub the mixture briskly all over the body. It will be messy, but marvellous, for sloughing off dead cells and revitalising sluggish, dull skin. Lie back in the bath and relax. You'll emerge feeling wonderfully glowing and relaxed.

Hint: Place a plug strainer — readily available from hardware stores — over the bath plug, so as not to clog the drains!

LAVENDER NOURISHING CREAM

Although this nourishing cream is particularly good in winter, it can be used for cracked heels and rough skin all year round.

1 cup aqueous cream
½ cup almond oil
1 cup English lavender leaves and flowers
2 teaspoons wheat germ oil

Warm the aqueous cream, almond oil and lavender together in a double boiler and simmer for 20 minutes, stirring occasionally. Strain and add the wheat germ oil. Mix well. Pour into a sterilised screw-top jar. Use lavishly!

LAVENDER AND CUCUMBER MASK

Lavender's astringent qualities combine beautifully with the soothing, deeply cleansing action of cucumber in this mask.

1 cup cucumber
1 cup lavender

Blend the cucumber and lavender together in a food processor. Lie back in a hot bath and pack the mixture over face and neck. Leave on for 10 minutes. Rinse off with warm water.

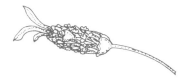

> ❧ HANDY HINT
> Tuck fresh lavender sprigs under your pillow to help you sleep.

LAVENDER HAIR RINSE

This rinse is excellent for oily hair, scalp itchiness or dryness. It is deeply cleansing, and can replace a conditioner occasionally. English lavender (*L. angustifolia*) is best here.

2 cups fresh English lavender leaves and flowers
2 litres water
½ cup apple cider vinegar
1 litre warm water

Boil the lavender leaves and flowers in 2 litres water for 10 minutes. Leave to stand and cool until pleasantly warm. Add the apple cider vinegar and 1 litre warm water.

Pour into the basin and use as a final rinse after shampooing the hair. Massage well into the scalp and comb gently through the hair. Dry briskly with a warm towel.

> **❧ HANDY HINT**
> Rub a restless baby's pillow or mattress with fresh lavender leaves to soothe and calm him.

Lavender bath soap

Lovely as a gift — even lovelier to spoil yourself — this is quickly and easily made and is excellent for oily, problem skin. The strong scent of English lavender is best here.

2–3 cakes plain baby soap or other plain soap (to make 4 cups)
1 cup English lavender leaves and flowers, chopped
1 cup boiling water
3 tablespoons lavender flowers and buds stripped from their stems
1 teaspoon lavender essential oil
a little mauve food colouring

Have ready several small dishes lined with plastic wrap. Grate the soap into a saucepan. Meanwhile boil the cup of chopped lavender leaves and flowers in the water for 10 minutes. Cool for 10 minutes, then strain. Add to the grated soap and gently boil for 5 minutes, stirring all the time.

Stir in 3 tablespoons lavender flowers and buds stripped from their stems, the lavender essential oil and, if desired, 2 or 3 drops of mauve food colouring. Stir well and pour into the moulds. Leave to set. Once set, remove the soap from the moulds and with a sharp knife trim the rough edges. Wrap in greaseproof paper and store for 1 month before using.

LAVENDER CELLULITE OIL

This can be used as an all over massage oil for loosening cellulite and is best used just before a bath so that it can continue its work with the hot water as you lie back and soak.

1 cup almond oil
½ cup chopped English lavender leaves and flowers
6 cloves, lightly crushed
1 tablespoon rosewater
2 teaspoons wheat germ oil
about ½ teaspoon lavender essential oil

Warm everything together, except for the essential oil, in a double boiler for 20 minutes with the lid on. Stir well every now and then. Strain and cool. Add the lavender essential oil and pour into a bottle with a screw top. Massage into the thighs, using circular movements. To warm the oil before use, stand the bottle in a jug of hot water until pleasantly warm.

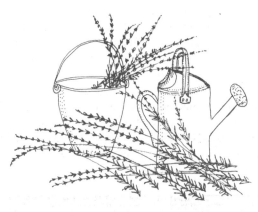

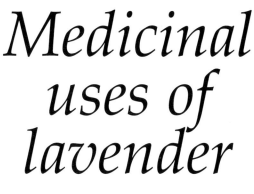

Medicinal uses of lavender

R*emember: Always consult your doctor before starting a home treatment.*

Over the centuries lavender in various forms has proved itself as an effective treatment for various ailments, and its remarkable properties are bound to receive further scientific validation in the years to come. It appears in many natural treatments, often taken as a tea, or used externally as a compress, lotion, massage cream or oil. Medicinally it seems the English lavender *(Lavandula angustifolia)* is the best species to use.

❧ Standard brew tea

This tea can be sipped to soothe a *tension headache, dizziness, nausea, anxiety, nervousness, muscular tension, indigestion, flatulence, bad breath, depression, sleeplessness* and *hyperactivity*. Many of our grandmothers made it for *rheumatic aches and pains, gout, arthritic joints, stiff muscles* and *cramps in the legs* and I find myself taking the tea for *insomnia* and wake next morning free of backache and having been free of cramps during the night.

¼ cup fresh lavender leaves and flowers
1 cup boiling water

Pour the boiling water over the lavender and stand for 5 minutes, then strain. Sweeten with a little honey if preferred or add a squeeze of lemon juice. I like it best on its own.

❧ Lavender lotion

This simple and soothing lotion is an excellent wash for *sunburn, grazes, itchiness, inflammation, infected cuts, mild burns* and *insect bites and stings*, as lavender has analgesic properties.

2 cups fresh lavender leaves
2½ litres water

Boil the fresh leaves in the water for 10 minutes. Stand aside, cool and then strain. Keep the excess in the fridge. Use this fragrant brew as a wash or dab on as a cleansing lotion, or decant into a bottle with a spray gun and spray on frequently to relieve the pain and heat of sunburn. Use as a freshener over the face, neck and arms on a hot day.

🕊 Lavender massage cream

I am never without this superb cream for *aches* and *itches*, *cramps* and *sprains* and it is simply lovely massaged into aching heels and calf muscles after a long hike.

1 cup aqueous cream
1 cup lavender leaves and flowers
6 drops lavender essential oil
2 teaspoons wheat germ oil

Warm the aqueous cream and lavender leaves and flowers gently together in a double boiler for 20 minutes. Strain out the flowers and leaves, and add the lavender essential oil and wheat germ oil. Mix well and pour into a sterilised screw-top jar.

🕊 Lavender compress

Never underestimate the soothing qualities of lavender over a *bruise* or *sprain*, or *aching joint*. I use the big blind lavender *(L. x allardii)* for this as its big fragrant leaves soften beautifully in hot water.

several lavender sprigs
boiling water

Pick enough sprigs to cover the area. Strip their leaves. Cover with boiling water for 5 minutes or enough to thoroughly soften them. Scoop out, and apply wet to the area. Cover with a towel and relax. I warm the towel by placing a hot water bottle over it. Relax for 15 minutes.

> 🕊 HANDY HINT
> A dab of lavender oil on the temples will soothe a headache.

🍃 Lavender steam inhaler

Blocked sinuses, colds, flu and *nasal congestion* are greatly relieved by steaming over a large basin of lavender brew. As a bonus your skin will emerge soft and clean with fewer wrinkles.

6 sprigs lavender
2 litres boiling water
4 drops Eucalyptus oil
2 drops lavender oil

Immerse the lavender in the boiling water and add the Eucalyptus oil and lavender oil. Make a tent with a towel over the head, bend over the steaming bowl and inhale the steam, keeping the eyes closed. Do not do this if you have thread veins.

🍃 Aromatherapy

The ancient Greek, Roman and Egyptian medicine men were well aware of lavender's tonic and sedative properties and made frequent reference to its therapeutic and beautifying attributes. In the twelfth and thirteenth centuries it was used to treat *colds* and *coughs, plagues, poor circulation, heart and liver ailments* as well as *apoplexy, epilepsy* and *mental derangements*.

Today distilled essential oil of lavender is still being used to treat these ailments. Its *antiseptic* and *antispasmodic* properties, too, have been added to its remarkable list of abilities. Lavender oil finds its place on many a modern bathroom shelf: apply it neat to *bites, stings* and *burns,* add a drop or two to a bath for a hyperactive child, a distraught teenager and her equally upset mother, and use it as a panacea for everything from *flu* to *nausea, headaches* to *gout, menopause* to *shingles*! And it smells glorious!

Lavender for fragrance

The rich fragrance of lavender is not only soothing and revitalising, but is very effective in repelling rats, mice, fleas, flies and even fishmoths from the house. I remember my grandmother placing sprigs and sachets of lavender richly scented with lavender oil bought in small bottles from the chemist, under cupboards, behind bookshelves, into drawers and even tucked up behind the sofa and kitchen sink. Rats and mice hate the smell of lavender and small balls of cottonwool soaked in lavender oil wiped along the skirting, window frames and doorsteps will deter many a mouse who dares to enter!

LAVENDER POT POURRI

This is my favourite recipe and probably all-time best seller should you be lucky enough to find it in the shops! I have a whole series of gift items made with this recipe: small sachets for the car, large sachets for the linen cupboard and flat sachets for behind books. To dry lavender, spread it out thinly on newspaper in the shade. Mince the lemon peel while it is fresh, spread it out on a metal tray and dry it in the sun.

10 cups dried French lavender leaves and flowers (or any lavender)
2 cups minced dried lemon peel
1 cup cloves
1 cup cinnamon and cassia pieces
1 cup coriander seeds
½ cup allspice berries
2 cups finely chopped lavender stems
about 2 tablespoons lavender oil*

Mix the lemon peel with the spices and the lavender stems. Add the lavender oil. Tip everything into a large glass jar with a screw top. Shake daily, adding more oil and shaking again. Leave it to blend well for 1 week, then add more oil and the lavender leaves and flowers. Keep it sealed and shake up daily for another week, adding more oil as needed.

Fill bags with this pot pourri or stuff coat hangers or sachets, or put it in pretty bowls around the house. Remember to cover it at night to keep it dust free.

---

* This is not the lavender essential oil used in aromatherapy, but a pleasant synthetic blend bought from the chemist.

LAVENDER PEACE PILLOW

The perfect gift for insomniacs. I must have made thousands of these over the years and they have been taken all over the world as travel pillows. I find the most comfortable size is 40 x 25 cm.

Make an inner pillow of pure cotton. Stuff it with foam chips or a polyester fibre filler. Make a small flat sachet 18 x 12 cm and fill it with this mixture:

½ cup chopped dried lemon peel
½ cup cloves
1 tablespoon lavender oil
1 cup dried English lavender flowers, stripped of their stems
1 cup dried lavender leaves (Grandmother's old English lavender
  has the longest lasting scent)

Mix the lemon peel and the cloves and add the lavender oil. Keep sealed in a screw-top bottle. Shake daily. Add more oil. After 1 week add the dried lavender leaves and flowers. Add a little more oil and keep sealed for a further week remembering to shake up daily.

Fill the sachet with this fragrant blend and sew up the end. Tuck into the centre of the pillow surrounded by the stuffing and sew the end of the pillow closed. Make a pretty pillow slip the same size as the pillow, edged with lace if desired. Use a fresh, easily washable material of light lawn or fine cotton. Revive from time to time by adding more lavender oil to the lavender mixture.

> **❧ HANDY HINT**
> Dry your washing on a lavender hedge and fold flowers into your linen for fresh-smelling laundry.

LAVENDER ROOM SPRAY

I make this fresh frequently. It helps to keep flies and mosquitoes away and during the summer months seems to cool and freshen the room beautifully.

During winter I leave the pot simmering on the stove gently all day and open all the interleading doors so that the fragrance can permeate the whole house. This is a lovely way of getting rid of stale cooking smells, pet smells and lingering cigarette smoke, and of humidifying the air. Blind lavender *(L. x allardii)* or Dutch lavender *(L. angustifolia x dentata)* are best here.

10 sprigs lavender leaves and flowers
3 litres water
few drops lavender essential oil

Boil the sprigs of lavender leaves and flowers in the water for 20 minutes. Cool. Strain. Discard the lavender. Add a few drops of lavender essential oil. Pour into a spritz bottle with a pump action, and spray liberally and lavishly all over the room and all around while sitting out on the patio to keep mosquitoes away.

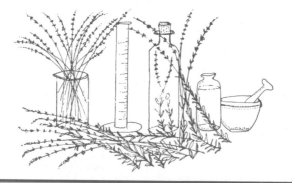

Companion planting

Lavender is a wonderful companion plant, keeping pests at bay with its marvellous insect-repelling properties.

Hedges of lavender protect other plants and are used extensively overseas in organic vegetable gardens. All the lavender varieties can be used with much success. My vegetable garden is surrounded by lavender — which I need to keep clipped as it tends to become very big — and I find I never need to spray the vegetables.

The lavender clippings are useful as a mulch all over the garden, deterring aphids, slugs and snails and keeping the whole garden healthy.

- A lavender mulch made from the clippings deters slugs, snails and beetles that attack lettuces.

- Use lavender clippings under strawberries instead of straw to keep millipedes at bay.

- Use clippings under ripening brinjals and tomatoes, and near onions, to keep them pest-free and healthy.

- Lavender alternated with fennel keeps aphids off the fennel.

- Lavender mulch keeps down mildew, especially under roses.

- Lavender clippings keep rose beetles at bay.

Lavender insecticides

As our environment becomes increasingly polluted, so it becomes more and more important to use natural insecticides to eliminate the need for harmful synthetic ones. Lavender fills this role admirably, and in various forms is a remarkably effective insect-repellent. Fresh lavender clippings may be used as a mulch or made into a brew and sprayed onto plants to repel garden pests; dried lavender made into sachets will deter fishmoths; lavender room spray will keep mosquitoes and flies at bay and fragrant lavender candles will keep the house mosquito-free in summer.

LAVENDER INSECT-REPELLING SPRAY

I use this particularly for aphids, mildew, rust and whitefly on house plants, vegetables and inside the dogs' kennels and baskets. Blind lavender *(L. x allardii)* and Dutch lavender *(L. angustifolia x dentata)* are excellent here.

½ bucket lavender twigs, leaves and flowers, roughly chopped
1 bucket boiling water
¼ bucket mixed rue and khakibos or marigold sprigs, roughly chopped
1 cup soap powder

Pour the boiling water over the leaves and stand overnight to draw. Next morning, strain. Dump the spent sprigs and leaves on the compost heap. Mix in the soap powder and stir well. Spray or splash onto plants.

This brew can be used to wash out bird cages, rabbit hutches and dog kennels.

LAVENDER INSECT-REPELLING CANDLES

I first began making candles 30 years ago when we had no electricity on our farm. I found lavender to be the most soothing fragrance for the children's bedrooms and I used combinations of citronella oil and lavender for midsummer when moths and mosquitoes were at their worst.

For a party table make several small candles. Stand them in a shallow glass dish filled with water and surround with masses of lavender flowers — the whole room will be scented, with not a mosquito or fly in sight!

6 white candles
1 teaspoon blue or purple wax crayon scrapings
2 tablespoons English lavender flowers and buds stripped of their stems
1 teaspoon lavender oil
1 teaspoon citronella oil

In an old saucepan, melt down the candles. Add a few scrapings from children's wax crayons — mauve or pale blue candles would complement the lavender well.

Add the rest of the ingredients and mix well. Pour into paper cups (not polystyrene) or milk cartons in which you have fixed a wick. Fix the wicks (bought at craft shops or use the wicks from the candles you melted down) by knotting the end through a hole in the carton. Seal it with masking tape underneath and tie the other end to a pencil that lies across the top of the cup.

Allow to set. Top up with more wax as a dimple is often left near the wick. Peel away the paper once the candle has set and trim off any rough spots with a sharp knife. Once you light it, add the odd drop of lavender oil to the melted wax under the flame.

INDEX